Just Thinking

Kevin Hadduck

ISBN: 978-1-967022-97-7

Fomite
Burlingon, VT
fomitepress.com

A Preface

This collection of brief essays may not directly address the raging political concerns of the moment, but they do, I hope, address some underlying issues of our national identity.

We have recently watched a genocidal, warmongering president pass the scepter to a new president who seems intent on two things: 1) carrying forward the Israeli agenda of genocide against Palestinians and wars of aggression against neighboring Arab states, all in service of a bipartisan foreign policy of regional and global economic dominance, and 2) creating a "Great Again" America defined by xenophobia, corporate greed, contempt for the poor and marginalized, religious bigotry, and nationalism. Religion and nationalism together create a toxic brew, a grave danger familiar to those who study history. While I write as a Christian, the very idea of a "Christian political party" or a "Christian nation" is anathema to me. I have told my wife that, if our government were formally to declare itself a "Christian country," I might have to find refuge in a foreign land. And here has come Trump, with strong hints of project 2025, a jingoistic nationalism, and a cabinet, like his predecessor's, full of imperialist, Zionist zealots who display utter contempt for international law.

It seems likely that nothing fundamental will change in our foreign policy, except perhaps the calculus of our imperial dominance; but much will change within our domestic policies. Leading up to the elections, many argued that, while the consequences of our actions "over there" may be tragic, we need urgently to focus on saving our democracy from Trumpian threats "here at home," pitting the rights and freedoms of marginalized people here against the very lives of people elsewhere. Having failed to elect a Democrat, we have traded a president who cloaked his genocidal foreign policy behind seductive promises of greater rights and freedoms here at home for a president whose imperial ambitions seem blatant and unapologetic, accompanied, of course, by his own set of seductive promises made to a different audience. Right and Left, many seem willing to concede the expediency of a genocide or, at least, the expediency of remaining mostly silent about it. I recall candidate Harris scolding a Palestinian protester for demanding an end to the genocide with this: "Keep saying that, if you want to see Trump elected!"

I will make this assertion: Who we are "over there" on foreign soil reflects precisely who we are, as a government and as a people, "here at home." In these little musings, I try to address that essential question: Who are we? I hope also to make an appeal: Moving forward, we will, as always, need courageous truth-tellers and courageous lovers of humanity. And we will need a bold humility.

1. We Expand Inward

Who are we, then, and who am I? What
is a human being? We gravitate toward simple,
politically expedient answers. We abuse the third-
person plural pronouns, they and them, with
facile generalizations about people we have not
troubled ourselves to understand.

Among the many insults that we humans
hurl at each other, this one has long impressed
me as among the most silly, yet also among the
most dehumanizing: "I can read you like a
book." Granted, we sometimes render ourselves
simple, by becoming predictable or obvious, but
I have never known a human being so readable
as even the most complex book. I recall studying
an introduction to a Chaucer text. The scholar
insisted that the Wife of Bath was more
interesting and complex than any actual, living
friend we might have. I do not recall the scholar's
name and do not care. In my imagination, he sits
eternally in a dim school-house corner, wearing a
dunce cap.

Our oversimplifying of each other as
individuals mirrors our stereotyping of others en
masse.

A mentor of mine* in disability services recently posted this biting comment from someone else: "A progressive's idea of diversity is everyone looking different but thinking exactly the same." I encounter that sort of pseudo-progressive perspective often. My many Arab friends find it especially offensive when Western activists come with the intention of rescuing them, not only from Western oppression, but from what many Westerners see as the Arab's self-inflicted suppression. Arabs, so go the stereotypes, are too emotional, prone to violence, illiberal, fiercely patriarchal, misogynistic, generally uneducated, overly religious, and (of course!) antisemitic. Thus, efforts to decolonize become self-serving attempts to recolonize, by a different, "progressive" set of Western values. It is interesting to me that among many young Muslim women, from conservative to liberal, the hijab and thobe are becoming symbols of cultural pride. Nonetheless, "they" need our intervention. We in the West labor under the delusion of our cultural, intellectual, and moral superiority.

After all, we know ourselves as beacons of freedom and democracy. We know who "they" are, as well, and how they really ought to be more civilized like us. We cannot leave them (poor victims!) to solve their own problems on their own. Such arrogance has informed the colonial mindset for centuries. We rightly admire those thinkers and activists who have enhanced our own understanding of human dignity, but we often fail to recognize the intellectual and moral accomplishments of "them," the others we ignorantly fear—and whose labor and resources we need at minimal cost. In other words, our finest discourse about human rights too often creates an elaborate fig leaf for our more carnal aspirations. We colonize, exploit, and extract at their expense.

First, we rob them of a fully human identity.

Definitions are problematic. An identity requires a definition, and a definition involves delineating the limits of a thing. Without mutually agreed upon definitions, our discourses would fall into confusion. Biologists apply, yet continually refine, their binomial nomenclature for all living things, facilitating an intelligible, progressive, and productive discourse. Every academic discipline proceeds on the basis of a discipline-specific lexicon. Even our casual conversations move forward, growing profound, silly, insightful, or confused, depending upon how well we understand and respect the limits of each other's definitions.

All of this, simple and obvious enough, nonetheless leads to a problem. What if the definitions we write for ourselves and for each other betray us? What if my self-definition is absurd or inordinately self-serving and, thus, abusive of others? What if my definition of you fundamentally misunderstands you and thus imposes narrow, debilitating limits on you? I remember telling my wife years ago, "We have settled into some rigid, simple understandings of each other; we no longer hear or see each other clearly enough. We need to reconceive each other more complexly." She and I have revisited that truth a number of times in our years together.

The problem often grows ruinous on a massive scale in social and political contexts, of course, when one group defines itself as, say, superior and more deserving or imposes narrow and denigrating limits on another, in order to suppress and control or to preserve an advantageous order by exclusion or elimination. My nominally Christian forefathers applied the label "savage" to indigenous faces, families, and cultures, and thus justified an insidious, yet calamitous genocide in the name of "manifest destiny." Some reject that word, genocide, as inapplicable, but as the old cliché goes, "The definition is in the details."

For the sake of some civil coherence, some law and order that allows us to live in mutually beneficial peace, we will accept a few definitions and the limits that inform them. For the sake of our mental and spiritual health as social beings, we will respect each other's familial, cultural, and religious or non-religious identities. I will not demand that everyone else be just like me—or even like me at all. I will not disparage definition, as if we can thrive alone or even define ourselves honestly and fully without acknowledging our deep-heart connectedness within community and, ultimately, with all of humanity.

For the sake of compassion, honesty, and justice, however, may we please remember a fundamental reality, perhaps the most salient truth about being human? Every human being expands inward beyond definition.

I carry this idea with me, everywhere, all the time: As a human being, you are far too deep, broad, and complex for any definable identity, other than "human." No gender, religion, ideology, skin color, race, ethnicity, culture, age, nationality, social cause, marital status, or disability can adequately encompass you. Not all such identities together can comprehend your immeasurably deep and complex Self.

So it is that the foreign populations we decimate with our bombs, bullets, and economic bullying, directly or by proxy, are comprised of immeasurably deep and complex Selves, whose dignity, value, and needs match our own. They, no matter how far away by miles or by culture, deserve no less than we do.

*Jane Jarrow. JanieOnLists@yahoo.com
[The_Last_Word] Jan 18, 2019

2. The Liar Went Home Smiling

Oh, but our differences, that is, our definitions, are problematic. We do not handle them well.

Political activists often ignore conventional wisdom about civility. Internet trolls, feeling invulnerable and suffering a bloated estimation of their intelligence and rhetorical power, ignore any and all wisdom about civility. Indeed, some who pass too easily as professional journalists function as highly paid trolls, leading their audience to a predetermined conclusion, plying guests with a repertoire of fallacious questions, and driving an interview toward a contrived "gotcha" moment, thus normalizing a more insidious sort of incivility.

We hear passionate laments about the loss of formalized respect and compassion in public discourse, and I do believe we suffer increasingly from rudeness and crudeness toward each other. I suggest, however, that much of our incivility rises from our bellies like a reflux, an inevitable response to one acidic problem deep within the bowels of our institutions—our governments, media, schools, churches, corporate and local boards, social service organizations, and yes, our homes.

The problem? We tolerate liars.

We so often elevate liars as candidates for every side of every aisle, and then we elect them to office, whereupon they appoint more liars into subservient roles. We then complain about those hypocrites across the aisle. God bless democracy.

At times our social etiquette compels us to keep quiet, speak with tact, remain courteous, genteel, decorous . . . for better and for worse. Such rules as we impose upon each other, given too much credence, grant corrupt leaders a huge advantage over a servile people. I have dutifully remained civil, for instance, while everyone else around the table likewise sat as dumbly as contented bovines, listening to the chairperson bloviate, intimidate, and tell egregious lies. Shhh.

One poor sap I worked for said this: "Here's how we fool the inspector." He then explained how to apply small amounts of expensive caulk, in order to hide large amounts of cheap spray foam in the pipe chases between floors of a hotel. Shhh.

Another slack-jawed yokel boasted about "teaching" his incredulous cabinet members how to "spin the data," in order to "lead board members to the right conclusion." Shhh.

An impressively urbane administrator threatened to fire a subordinate for accusing a colleague of lying. "You cannot do that!" he all but shouted. She had proof. Everyone knew the truth. None of that mattered. Shhh.

The liar went home smiling.

Centuries ago, a great voice said, "If it is possible, as far as it depends on you, live at peace with everyone." His mouth got him killed.

Not long before, another great voice scolded some religious leaders, "You are like whitewashed tombs, which look beautiful on the outside, but on the inside are full of dead men's bones and every impurity." And did he really whip the money changers in the Jerusalem temple? Or did he merely noodle them, with a condescending smile, a soft voice, hands clasped in front, head tilted to the side? Meh, if he did not go a bit berserk, then I question whether I should follow him. His mouth got him killed.

Odd, that, as Jesus was (by my dim lights) the consummate master of "speaking the truth in love."

Let me advance an idea: Necessary truth telling has never once in history caused a conflict.

King's "Letter from Birmingham Jail" beautifully displays the logic for truth-telling, even at great cost. No, a necessary truth has never ever created a conflict. Truth merely discovers a conflict already raging behind closed doors, uncovers the violence already occurring in the dark.

3. Invisible Heart of the Onion

I have failed to tell the necessary truth and have known the consequences of my cowardice.

I have spoken truth full of risk and known the cost of courage.

I have lost friendship on both accounts, been forced to change direction in my life, and felt in head and gut both the fire of shame and the flame of righteous indignation.

Faith rises in us as a fierce and defiant courage, standing confidently against the conventional wisdom which says, "Take care of yourself first; do not risk too much; follow your convictions only so far as keeping your wallet, your reputation, your office, or your blood allows." Keeping faith requires standing firm, even at the risk of losing—always at the risk of losing. The idea of keeping faith has no relevance, except in the context of threat and the risk of loss.

Before you choose to fight (by whatever means) for a righteous cause, for the necessary truth, first accept a few simple facts: You will suffer injury. You will suffer loss. You will suffer loneliness among friends. You will suffer betrayal. You will suffer a sense of guilt because you will cause someone else to suffer. In other words, at some level, in some way, you will suffer failure. You will be tempted to lose faith and retreat into quietude.

Tell me, please, how to find the invisible heart of the onion that is human motivation. Why do some keep faith, while some do not?

When I grow tired and wonder why I bother to fight, I am tempted to forget the riches that have come to me from standing firm and to consider losses only. Yet I know who I am. That knowledge, in fact, is the wealth I own for keeping faith.

The poet Rumi asks this: "What have I ever lost by dying?" Can I love that question, if I fear, too much, the answers?

4. Redirecting the Rush Hour Traffic

Let me offer a brief caution, something along the lines of a moral cost-benefit assessment, something more about the possibility of dying, perhaps.

Let sensitive mathematicians determine the relevance, if any, of chaos theory to our mundane lives. Let wide-eyed screenplay writers manipulate the plot lines of infinite possible futures. Let blunt-headed activists assume a simple cause-effect reality and rest their grand hopes on grand causes.

We catch the wind of voices from every direction, calling us, urging us, demanding that we make a difference. We try. We fail more often than not. We persevere or quit in frustration, but we know in our hearts that action and inaction alike have consequences, and humility precludes arrogant predictions. In fact, we do not know the untraceable, uncountable effects of our mere existence.

For all I know, the equivalent of a butterfly wing triggered the Big Bang, and World War 2 effectively began in a monster's mind when the price of a bread loaf in Berlin jumped by one pfennig. I do not know very far, but I expend a lot of breath praying, teaching, learning, and creating what effectual breeze I can by keeping my hands reasonably busy, reaching toward one good effect or another. I try.

I try; therefore, I believe.

We take a bold step of faith merely by stepping out of or into bed.

A moment approaches. We anticipate. We assess. We look left and right. We lean forward and lift one foot. Immediately, we hear the angry horns, the curses, the shrieking of rubber against the asphalt. We make choices, so this fool believes, and the consequences come roaring at us like rush-hour traffic.

We learn. And, as we must, we again take our step and then take our stand.

5. Puzzle Pieces

"Although every piece be true, the puzzle itself be false." Shakespeare

We tell the truth, but.

I can lie to you in a thousand ways. I can state a thousand facts and provide a hundred plausible fact claims and yet lie to you. I can frustrate an army of assiduous fact-checkers searching for a falsehood, and yet never tell the truth.

Sit down with me at a puzzle, with the pieces still in piles and the box-top picture displayed for reference. With great patience, careful observation, intuition, comparing and contrasting piece to piece and piece to picture, we conduct our particular test of all the details and slowly recreate the whole.

What if you know from the picture that our puzzle will display someone's fanciful vision of the Jabberwock? I will not have deceived you. You know the Jabberwock does not exist.

What if, on the other hand, we work together as teacher and student. You dutifully follow my procedural directions, respect my insights about how to determine the fitness of a piece, and eventually complete the picture on your own? This puzzle, by the way, tests your patience and your intelligence, presenting you with 10,000 complexly cut pieces, all adding up to a grand pictorial narrative of . . . .

What if, yet again, the picture on the box tells a false tale, a prejudiced understanding of a great historical narrative? What if the epic panorama presents a politically motivated distortion? Let's think big: Carrier-Belleuse and Gorguet's 402-foot "Pantheon de la Guerre," as reduced and reconfigured by MacMorris. Stand and salute! "Dulce et decorum est pro patria mori," says Horace.

Oh, step back with me instead and stand in awe of the original work! Forget the unacknowledged ugliness of savage colonial powers groveling in mutual self-destruction. "Dulce et Decorum Est," Wilfred Owen wrote, then died crossing the Sambre-Osie Canal.

6.The Voices I Hear
Your Voice

Whether social mores or religious rules allow us to hug, or merely to shake hands, or compel us to avoid touching altogether, let me say I love you while close enough to see clearly the color of your eyes. I do not so much grow tired of talking with you by voice chat, text, or email; I merely grow frustrated at not having that most wonderful option: speaking to you in person, friend facing friend. I want you close to me, near enough to hear your voice without the thinning, sharpening effect of electronics. Your voice comes as a joy to me, a deep solace, nonetheless, no matter how it comes, even when by the silent progress of a text message across my screen. Over time, even over great distance, I learn your voice and hear your voice among the patterns of your texting.

My Voice

I used to say, "I inherited a boot for a tongue; please forgive me if I step clumsily or kick you accidentally." My forthright wife has assured me, however, through years of hearing me stumble, that I have learned; my words do not so often outpace my brain or trample someone's heart. Indeed, I have worked hard to refine my voice, to soften my footfall, so to speak, and more skillfully choreograph the dance of words among my best intentions, my reasoning, and my passion. All of this assumes that I do, in fact, have a voice, not merely a speaking voice, as nearly everyone has, but a voice that carries some power, for better or worse, as, in fact, everyone has. But does everyone have a voice that carries some power? Can anyone, anyone at all, speak with power, or speak effectively to power? I will come back to those questions.

My Father's Voice

My father could not hear my voice. I stood always at the intersection of his poor hearing and his selective listening. Most of the time, I stood silently there, as speaking seemed rarely to correlate with being heard. Indeed, it seemed most often that speaking on my own behalf meant not being heard. I might sit next to him and speak directly to his ear, and he, with face contorted by annoyed frustration, might say to my mother sitting across the room, "I can't hear. What is he trying to say?" In a soft voice, she would repeat my words to him. At other times, astonishingly, he would hear a near whisper from me and accuse me of saying something inappropriate. "I know what I heard!" he would shout, my denials only fueling his anger.

Governments function this way, do they not? Especially those governments bent on silencing dissent. Whom they cannot seduce, they suppress.

The Friend's Voice

We are susceptible to seduction. Thus, Solomon tells us that we should prefer an honest slap on the face to a dishonest kiss on the cheek. "Faithful are the slaps by a friend, while the kisses of an enemy are profuse," he says, and "Just as iron sharpens iron, one friend sharpens another." The violent imagery in his metaphors suggests that he wrote from experience. It seems unlikely that anyone, unschooled by the messy, troublesome, and often painful realities of human relationships, would think to craft such startling proverbs.

We rightly disparage flatterers in general. We may grumble to each other about the most debonair flatterer and issue discreet cautions when we hear him working a potential victim. We have seen what happens when the silver-tongued predator turns his sweet, blood-warming language toward a naïve or needy youngster . . . blushes, goosebumps, rushes, and high hopes. We know his motives for praising what he does not truly love, so we dare not trust his grasping hands.

An aspiring writer confessed to me once that he wrote poetry "mostly because women like it." Unfortunately, he knows his craft just well enough to lure the most vulnerable.

An impish irony dances across the stage of that little drama. Why would I expose the falseness of a compliment? Why would I want to say, earnestly, "Those lovely things you say about me are not true," or "Thank you for the kind words and generous offer; now get lost, you unctuous toad-eater"? I might, in fact, enjoy the benefits of the flattery, and thus the rewards of my complicit acquiescence.

Ah, "there's the rub," I tell myself, as I consider the self-murder of my integrity. A kiss comes with the promise of a tangible reward, while a slap on my flatterer's face might expel me from my own fantasy. Or put me out of favor with my beloved political party.

I do mean all of this, of course, as a metaphor for our politics, our political affiliations, and our politicians. We dare not trust them too much, nor even trust ourselves too much, no matter what promises they make to us.

The Voice Speaking Truth to Power

We need voices speaking truth about Power, about corrupt leaders, institutions, corporations, and governments. Even more, however, we need voices speaking truth to Power. Truth about Power and truth to Power are not the same. I speak truth to Power if the Power poses a threat to me, that is, if I risk something substantial by facing that threat and speaking a dangerous truth into the ear of Power. On a small scale, I have spoken truth to Power and lost a job and my health as a consequence. Soon after losing my job, my doctors handed me a twofold diagnosis: viral infection of my central nervous system and multiple sclerosis (MS). They suggested that the stress from that year of conflict contributed to the onset of both diseases, as intense stress suppresses the immune system.

While I would rather experience again the year of physical hell that came with the viral infection than face again the stress of fighting with corrupt leaders, I have no regrets. I can reflect on those years and affirm that my moral cost-benefit assessment was correct. I followed my conscience, knowing only partially what the consequences might be, but not what they would actually be.

We all know the words of Cassius, from Shakespeare's "Julius Caesar." In fact, we see and hear them quoted frequently by partisans following every conceivable banner—and every tyrant and demagogue:

> And why should Caesar be a tyrant then?
> Poor man! I know he would not be a wolf
> But that he sees the Romans are but sheep.

He were no lion were not Romans hinds. One zealot's tyrant is another's messiah. Our most recent national debates about presidential candidates proved to some folk what some other folk already knew: There is, apparently, no insurmountable contradiction between aggressively pursuing a genocide, on the one hand, and being Democrat or Republican, on the other. Can we work together and find a more humane path forward, one that does not dismiss outrage over genocide as the self-righteous pursuit of "moral purity"? Can we not be sheep?

The Voice of Love

Let me paraphrase St. Paul: If I do not have love, I have nothing. If I do not have love, I am nothing.

Given the absolute prominence that Paul gives to love, I think it fair to follow his logic further by saying that without love, there is nothing of value—no Goodness, no Truth, no Beauty—no Justice. We practice "speaking the truth in love," as he says, or we speak with no good purpose and to no good effect, even if we do indeed speak truth to Power. In saying this, I fear being misunderstood by those who equate "love" with all things sweet, nice, pleasant, and easy. I do not make that equation. Love may not, does not, always mean compromise, conciliation, or reconciliation. Indeed, love compels us to speak truth to Power boldly and forcefully, to risk our welfare, our health, even our lives. Love compels us to speak truth to

Power, no matter who is in Power, even if it happens to be the "lesser evil" of our choosing.

We read our nation's history and feel a deep admiration for those who spoke truth to Power and suffered the consequences. We aspire to emulate them—or not. Admiration alone costs nothing.

How often these days do we hear voices saying, indignantly, "I refuse to feel ashamed of anything bad that my forefathers did. I was not there; I did not participate!" I do not, by the way, hear those same voices, obedient to their own logic, saying, "I refuse to feel proud of anything good my forefathers did. I was not there; I did not participate!" This defensive argument, "I was not there!" it seems to me, is most fundamentally a failure of that love we call empathy (and a failure of Reason). It strikes me as an expression of moral cowardice as well. Or perhaps it betrays contentment with the current "lesser evil" of our choosing, so long as he makes promises to our liking. So long as we can celebrate the bright glories of our past, unencumbered by our darker memories or by the darkness of our own, present shadow.

Over the years, reading about the British Empire and the other, Western, "democratic" colonial powers, I changed. What had passed as mere, boring facts of history when I was very young began to leave me astonished and appalled. All the facts not given, the stories not told, the hidden truths that fill the vast gaps of an old and self-aggrandizing fiction, are facts of the utter barbarity, brutality, and monstrous arrogance of the British powers—and the Belgian, French, German, and American. How ironic that Germany, in the decades leading up to Hitler's rise and ghastly crimes, was broadly considered to embody the highest, most advanced culture, intellectually, artistically, politically, and socially.

For years now, I have felt almost frantic, wanting to run around saying, not "I am sorry," as if I were personally responsible for my country's past sins, but, instead, "I love you, I love you, tell me how to love you," as if I were waking up from a nightmare of losing loved ones I had failed even to recognize and, thus, had never known.

7. We Are Democratic, Aren't We?

We say we want some form of democracy, theoretically, but we all want it to be so much simpler and easier than it is. We want it, but only of, by, and for those people who generally agree with us or, most immaturely, for those who approve of us, the achievement of which means the end of democracy. I am a Christian; he is a Muslim; she is an atheist. Indeed, I live in a multifaceted mash-up of cultures, confronting almost daily a multiplicity of lifestyles and a kaleidoscope of socio-political beliefs. If we pay close attention to each other, we discover that our differences often run deep, even when we look alike.

I will not insult myself or you by asserting the facile, disingenuous nonsense du jour that partially defines my generation, "Oh, it doesn't matter what you believe about god, or if you believe in a god at all, so long as you embrace diversity and practice tolerance." My beliefs matter to me. Your beliefs matter to you. I will not insult the work you put into discovering, challenging, reformulating, and even changing your beliefs. I will assume the best about you, by assuming that you have worked very hard and for many years at assembling your own mind and settling your own heart.

Indeed, we bring our beliefs, of whatever sort (religious or non), to the negotiating table and the voting booth, and we mean business. None of us gets to tell the other that his beliefs have no relevance and that, therefore, he must leave his beliefs at the door—or out of the public square. In every context, our beliefs define and direct us and therefore remain with us in situ. On the other hand, always on the other hand, and we have so many hands.

Embracing diversity and tolerance does not go far or deep enough, in part because we cannot honestly embrace or even tolerate every diversity finding its way into our mutual governance. Consider the white supremacist, for instance. We pale at the thought of him gaining power in our government, but there he is, cheered on by hordes of like-minded sycophants. So how do we love each other now, while also, doggedly, speaking truth to Power? That question finds its complicated and frightening answers as we confront a prior question: What is love? That seemingly impossible question really is this: What is love within our current circumstance? Speaking truth to Power is challenging enough, but what does it mean to love in the face of Power and under the abusive weight of Power?

For the better part of five weeks, following the devastating tornado of May, 2007, I helped prepare and coordinate groups of volunteers, as they entered Greensburg, Kansas. One day, a group began cleaning up the debris of a home but stopped their work when they discovered white-supremacist literature and paraphernalia in the owner's basement. Why should they help a moral cretin who clung to such reprehensible beliefs? They did not persuade easily, but they came to understand something essential: their own professed beliefs required that they accept the role of good Samaritan and show kindness, even to that man —that they love even that man (to put a specifically Christian asterisk on it).

I know that I am not solving any political problems here; rather, I am trying to orient myself to what seems to be that essential, first, but impossible question: What is love? What does love compel us to do? We do say, albeit imprecisely, "Our diverse beliefs don't matter in a crisis. We must show compassion to everyone just the same." Indeed, we must; so I believe, and I have my reasons for believing so. You are welcome to believe otherwise, but if your ass falls into a ditch, I will help you pull it out, just the same.

www.ingramcontent.com/pod-product-compliance
Lightning Source LLC
Chambersburg PA
CBHW032057040426
42335CB00036B/484